DISNEY's
HOW · TO · DRAW
Bambi

Illustrated by
David Pacheco
Diana Wakeman

Walter Foster

The Making of *Bambi*

The movie *Bambi* is based on the book by Felix
Salten. The release of *Bambi* in 1942 marked a
departure from the comic Silly Symphonies and fairy
tales that had made the Disney
Studios famous. Moviegoers
young and old responded with
delight. Here was an animated
movie filled with all the
excitement, pathos, and humor
of a live-action film.

Here is one of
the original
Bambi movie
posters from
1942.

The story of *Bambi* is simple enough. A young deer experiences joy and sorrow while coming to maturity in the forest. Disney hoped to capture the beauty of nature with animation, while entertaining his audience with appealing characters and dramatic situations. In each regard, *Bambi* is a success.

This exciting hunting scene proves that animation can be dramatic as well as humorous.

The initial sketches for Bambi ranged from cartoony deer to photorealistic deer, from lamb-like fawns to majestic stags with rippling muscles. The final Bambi is a winning combination of realism and caricature. "Little pumpkin-head" is what many of the Disney artists affectionately dubbed him.

Notice how Bambi developed from these early character sketches to the final version.

Disney artists studied live deer in order to achieve realism in their drawings for *Bambi*.

The character of Thumper underwent similar changes. The original Thumper was drawn as a wizened old jackrabbit. As time went on, he became younger and younger.

There was less emphasis on realism in the drawing of Flower, the skunk. Walt Disney decided that audiences might not be sympathetic to a skunk character, and so every effort was made to make him as appealing as possible. That is why he was given bright blue eyes!

Drawing Techniques

Drawing Bambi and his friends can be fun and rewarding. With a little patience and practice, you will soon be producing successful drawings of your own.

Most characters are based on simple round and oval shapes. Using a light, continuous motion, sketch around and around until you've made a circle or oval that is the correct shape. Also practice drawing curves with smooth strokes. You may then erase any stray lines for a clean look. Try sketching a variety of sizes, or join shapes together to create new shapes.

One of the most important things to remember is to begin with a line of action. Draw a ball for the head and a curving line to represent the body. This is what gives your character movement and life. The line of action should flow naturally and smoothly.

It's useful to transfer the outline of your drawing onto tracing paper. This gives you a silhouette that reflects the character's proportions and shows if you have created a clear, strong pose. A good silhouette leads to a good finished drawing.

Once you've drawn your character, carefully erase the line of action and other construction lines to clean up your drawing. Now you're ready to color Bambi.

Bambi's Head

This three-quarter view of Bambi's head not only shows depth and form, but also conveys his personality. Knowing the character's inner feelings helps to achieve a successful drawing.

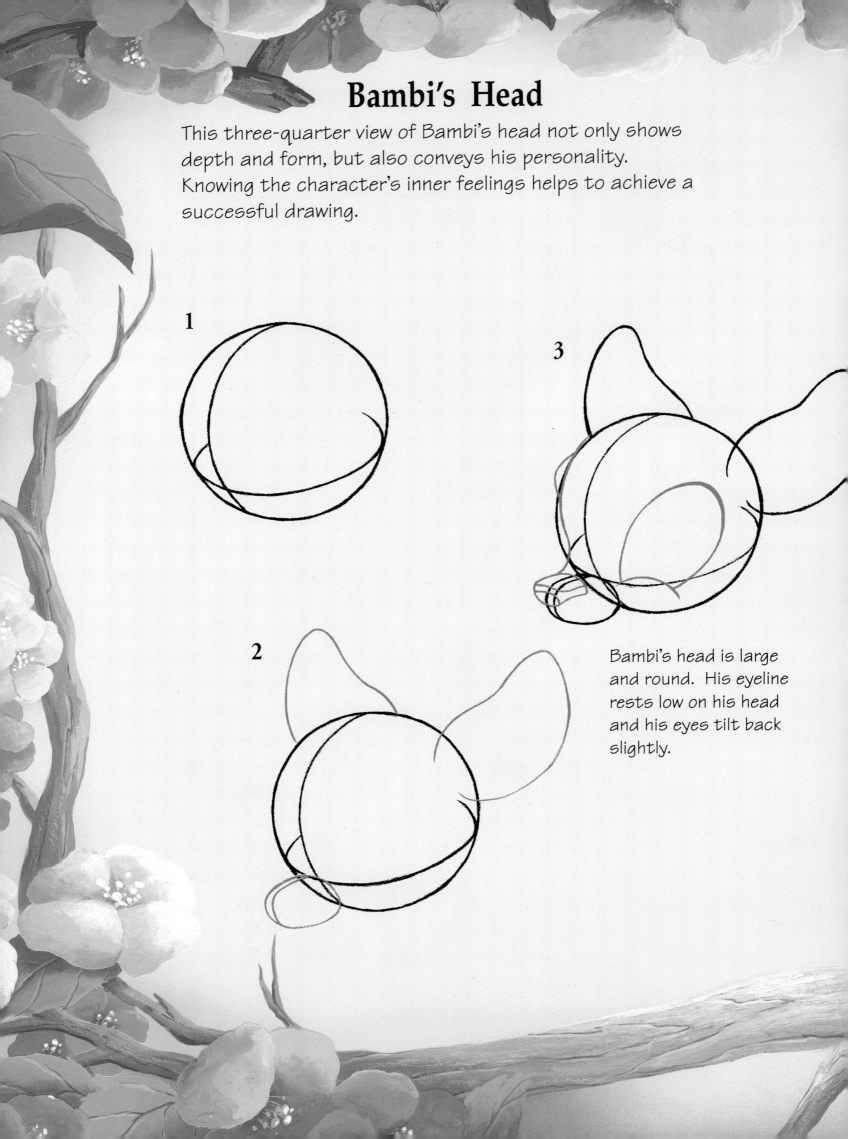

1

2

3

Bambi's head is large and round. His eyeline rests low on his head and his eyes tilt back slightly.

4

5

Bambi's ears are large and set
toward the back of his head.
Keep his mouth tiny, but be
sure he has a cheerful grin.

6

Bambi's Expressions

Although Bambi is a cartoon deer, he comes to life with realistic, childlike expressions. His small muzzle and wide eyes make a variety of expressions available to the artist.

shy

determined

thoughtful

happy

perplexed

friendly

surprised

frightened

content

sleepy

Bambi Standing

Young Bambi has a magical charm that has won the hearts of several generations. Use what you've learned about drawing Bambi's head and facial expressions when drawing his body.

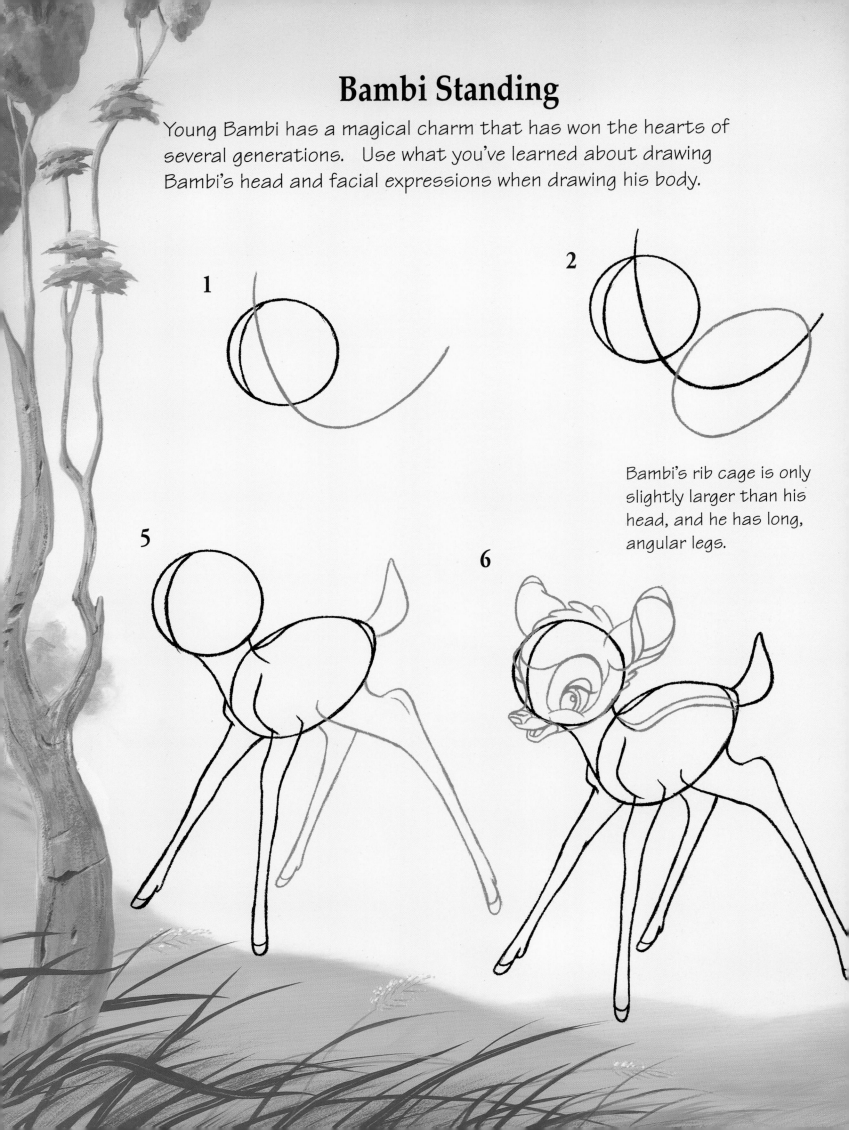

1

2

Bambi's rib cage is only slightly larger than his head, and he has long, angular legs.

5

6

3

4

7

8

Bambi's spots are rounded rectangles
that follow the line of his back and the
curvature of his body.

Bambi's Action Poses

Bambi's personality and mannerisms can be enhanced with the right action. Practice drawing the poses illustrated and then create some new ones of your own.

Thumper's Head

Making a character believable is the key to producing a good drawing. This three-quarter view helps bring Thumper to life.

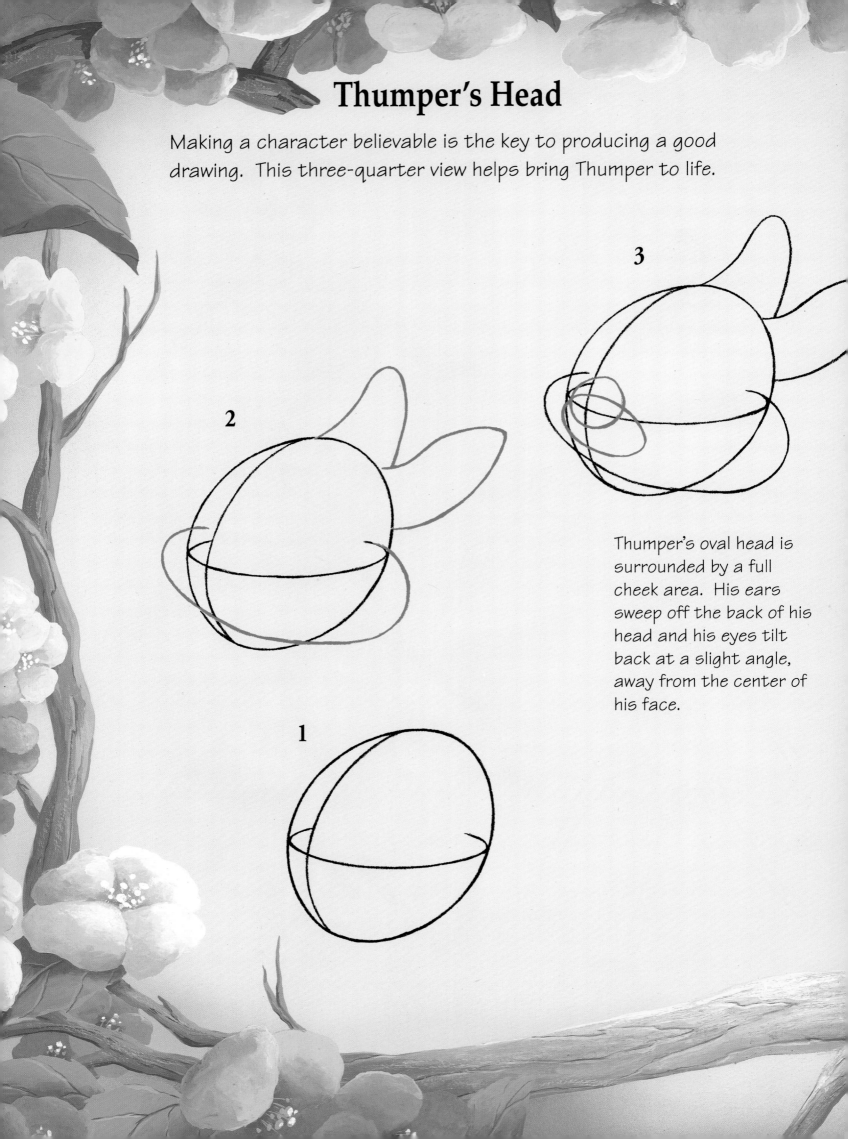

3

2

1

Thumper's oval head is surrounded by a full cheek area. His ears sweep off the back of his head and his eyes tilt back at a slight angle, away from the center of his face.

4

5

6

Thumper Standing

Thumper is made up of soft, curving lines with no sharp angles. He has a full, fluffy chest and oversized feet. Keep his ears and front paws relatively small.

3

4

7

8

Thumper's Action Poses

The action poses below show the wide range of movement Thumper has. Like a real rabbit, Thumper uses his large hind feet to spring into action.

Flower's Head

Flower's innocence and bashfulness are qualities that make him so endearing. Use the three-quarter view to bring out the subtle curves of his forehead and his petite nose and muzzle.

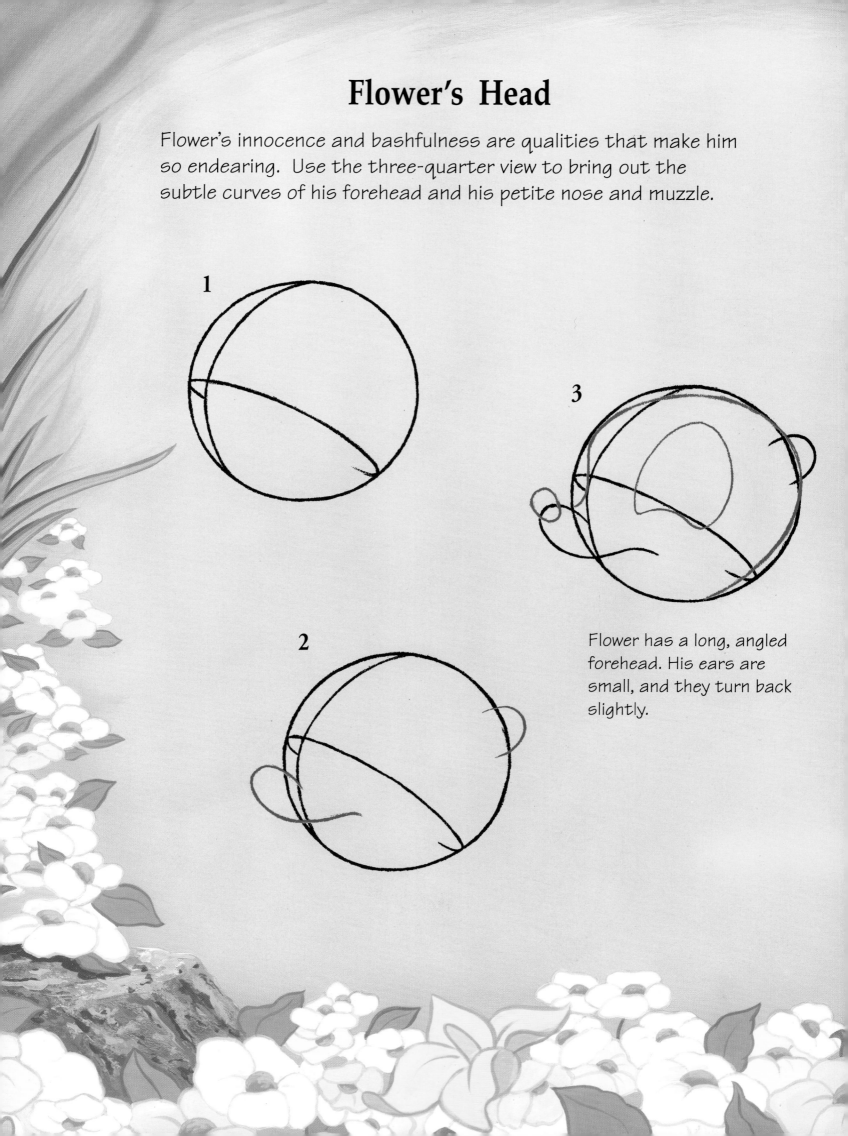

1

3

2

Flower has a long, angled forehead. His ears are small, and they turn back slightly.

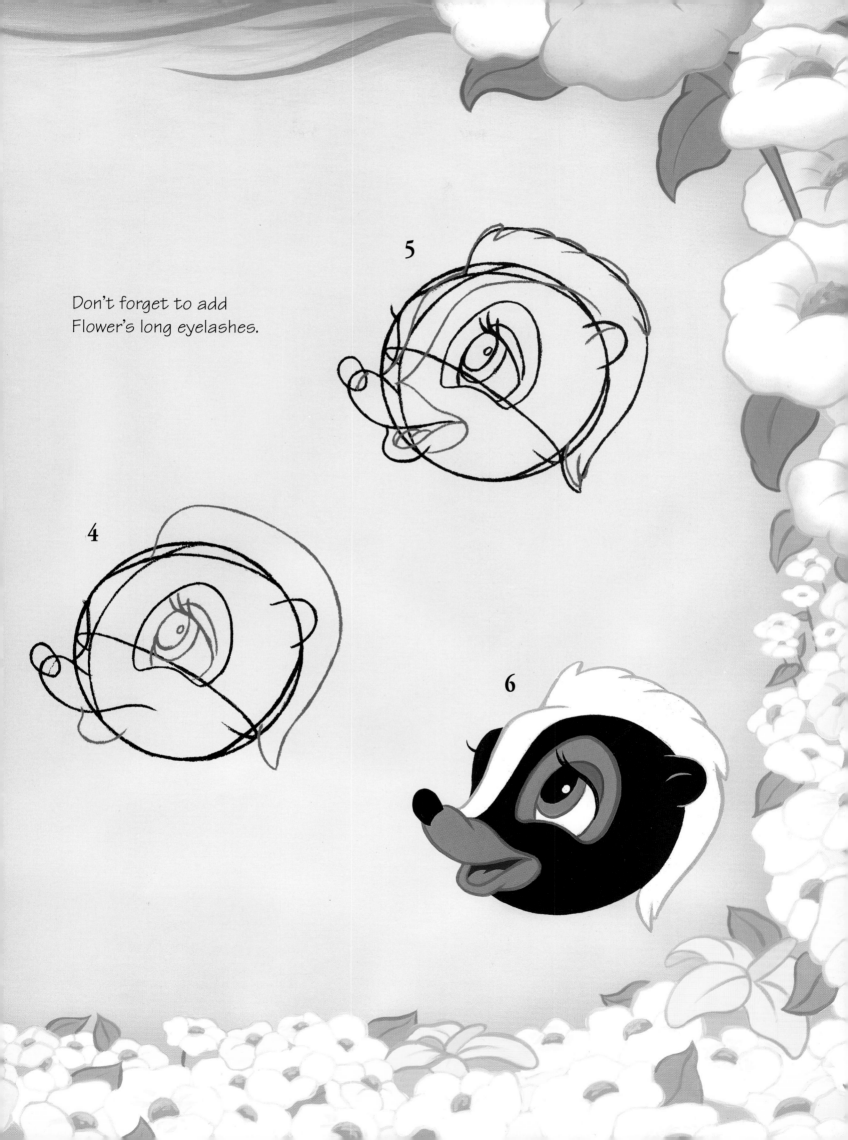

Don't forget to add
Flower's long eyelashes.

5

4

6

Flower Standing

Flower has a pear-shaped body. His babylike hands are round, with small, short fingers, and his tail is a little longer than his body.

3

4

7

8

Flower's Action Poses

Remember that Flower is a very timid, sweet skunk whose poses should reflect these qualities. See if your drawings do, too.

Friend Owl Standing

Friend Owl is short and stout, with large eyes that reflect his wisdom. Remember that he has a heavy body and short legs. Try to convey this feeling of weight when drawing him.

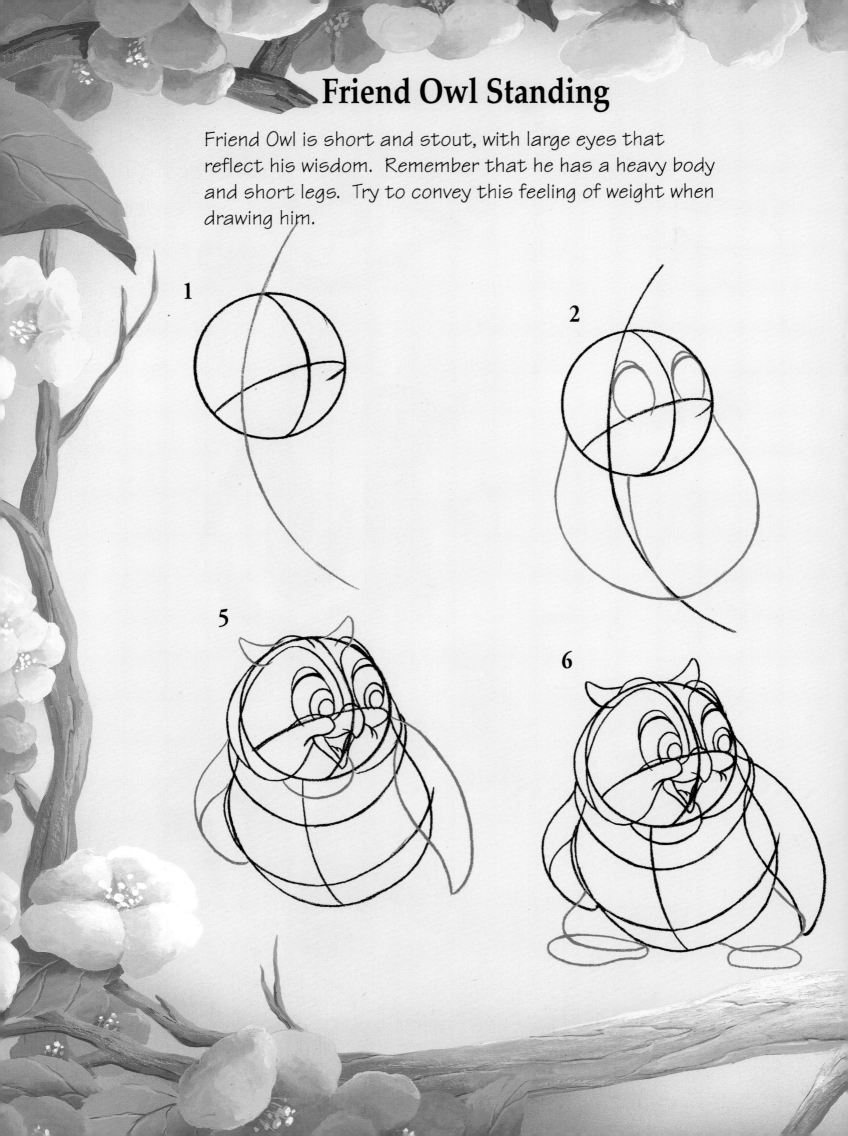

1

2

5

6

3

4

7

8

Friend Owl's Action Poses

Since Friend Owl is an animated character, he can use his wings to fly or to imitate the action of human arms and fingers.

Adult Bambi's Head

Adult Bambi is drawn very differently from baby Bambi. His once-large forehead is now shorter and flattened with subtle, long curves.

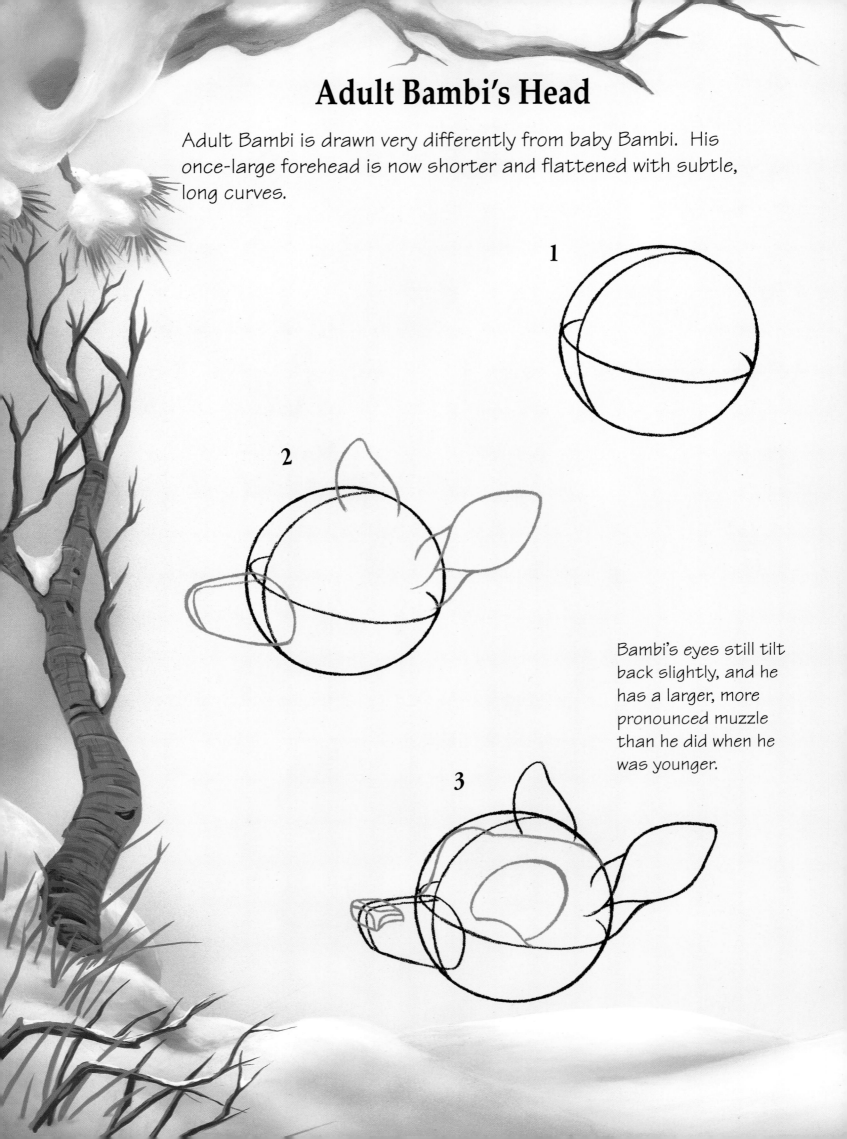

Bambi's eyes still tilt back slightly, and he has a larger, more pronounced muzzle than he did when he was younger.

6

Bambi's antlers are a little longer than his head, with two prongs on each.

5

4

Adult Bambi Standing

The adult Bambi is drawn in a more realistic fashion. His body mass is greater than when he was a baby, and he is a much sturdier and more self-confident character.

3

4

7

Now that he's grown, Bambi has more muscle tone and definition in his limbs.

8

Forest Friends

Secondary characters play an important role in completing a situation or adding to an emotional moment. Here are some more of Bambi's forest friends.

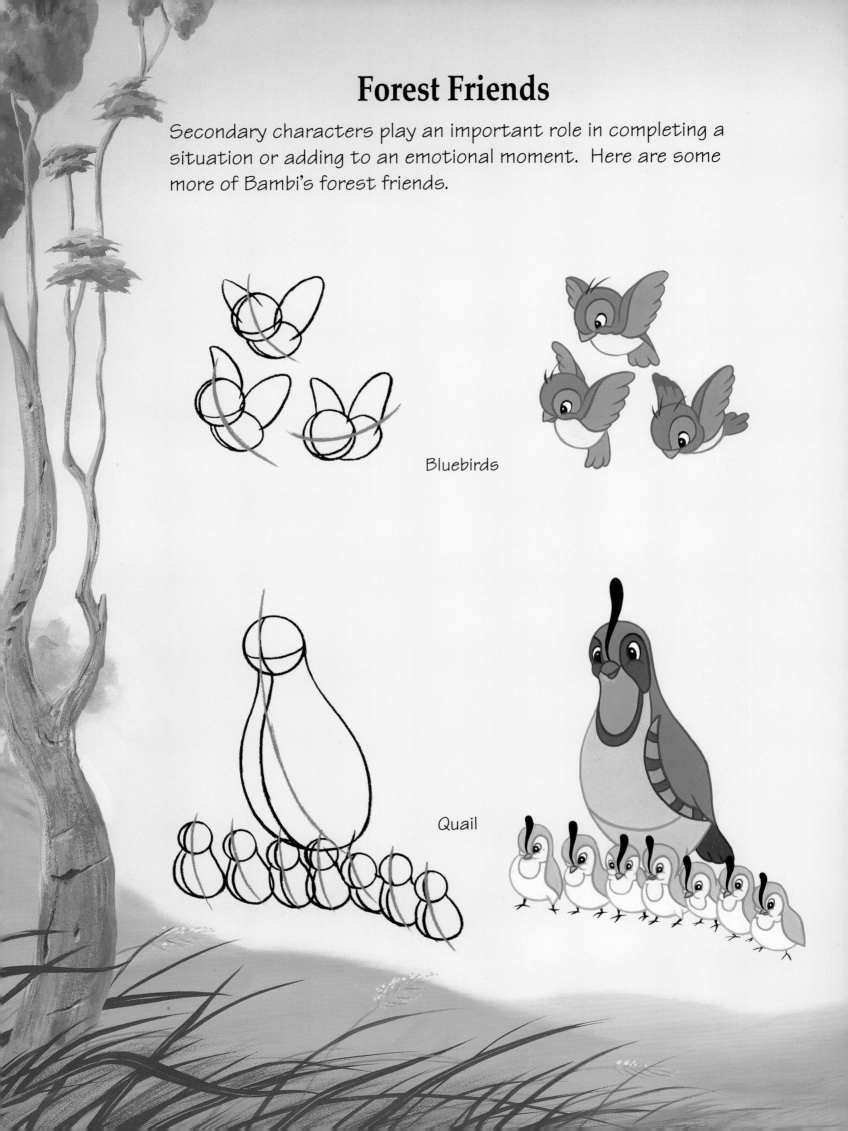

Bluebirds

Quail

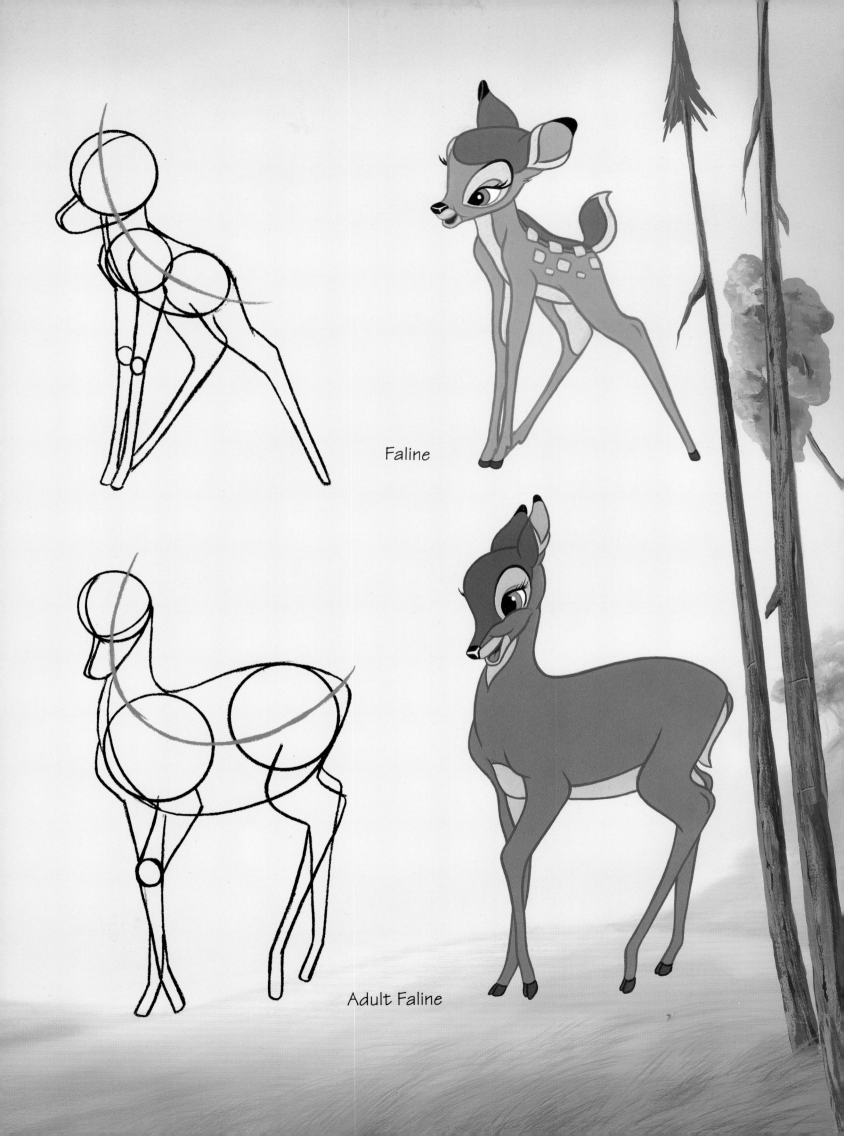

Faline

Adult Faline

Forest Friends

Squirrel

Duckling

Opossum

Chipmunk

Mouse

Thumper's Mother

Forest Friends

Adult Bird

Mole

Raccoon

Miss Bunny

Prince of the Forest

Finishing Techniques

You can finish your drawing with a variety of media. A finished drawing doesn't necessarily mean color. Some artists like the look and feel of graphite. You can use the side of a pencil to shade your illustration.

Colored pencils can be one of the easiest media to use. They're fast and economical and produce beautiful results.

Watercolors give a soft look to the character. A feeling of fantasy and romance can be conveyed with this medium.

You may also want to finish your drawing with charcoal or pastels. Paints and colored pencils are other options. Notice how each of these techniques gives a different look to the same drawing.

Charcoal, or graphite, gives a very artistic look to your drawing. Creating shaded tones with only blacks and whites helps you achieve depth and volume in the character.

In this book, the paintings were painted with gouache to achieve a bright, flat look.